I CAN'T
COOK
BOOK

Published by Brolga Publishing Pty Ltd
ABN 46 063 962 443
PO Box 12544, A'Beckett St, VIC, 8006, Australia
email: admin@brolgapublishing.com.au

National Library of Australia Cataloguing-in-Publication entry:
    Welling, Rose.
    I Can't Cook Book / Rose Welling
    2nd ed.
    9781925367249 (pbk.)
    Includes index.
    Cooking.
    641.512

Printed in Indonesia
Cover by David Khan
Typeset by Esther van Doornum

I CAN'T COOK BOOK

Rose Welling

Contents

Contents

Foreword

Moved out of home?

Wife, mother or significant other no longer around to cook for you?

All restaurant and cafe food has begun to taste the same, the phone bill has come in, you've fallen behind with the rent and you can't even afford a cheeseburger let alone a decent bit of Chinese nosh or a takeaway curry.

"I Can't Cook!" you say?

Well then, it's time to make friends with your kitchen. You're reading this aren't you?

And believe me, if you can read you can cook.

It might not be the stuff of gourmets who like to indulge in toasted peacock tongues and the like, it probably won't get you a spot on one of those telly shows where they toss up dishes using all sorts of ingredients you haven't got in the pantry.

But turn the page, follow the instructions and you'll be able to make a meal or two that is decent enough to share with a few friends and isn't going to cost a fortune.

Conversion Charts

Getting the right quantity and cooking at the right temperature are essential for any cook. Follow these easy to use charts and you'll be cooking in no time.

Common Cooking Terms

Baste: Spoon hot dripping or marinade over meat and vegetables while they are cooking.

Blanch: Place food in boiling water, and bring quickly back to the boil, then drain and plunge into ice cold water then drain again.

Blend: Mix a dry and moist ingredient to a smooth paste.

Cream: Beat butter (usually with sugar) until light and fluffy.

Dice: Chop food into small cubes.

Glaze: Brush scones, breads, etc. with a liquid.

Julienne: Cut vegetables into fine strips.

Marinate: Soak food in a mixture, such as a combination of vinegar, oils, soy sauce, honey, etc.

Par boil: Partly cook food in boiling liquid.

Puree: Mash, sieve or blend food in a food processor.

Saute: Toss food gently with butter or oil and flavourings over heat.

Shred: Cut into long narrow strips.

Sear: Brown surface of meat quickly.

Sift: Put dry ingredients through strainer or sifter to aerate and remove any lumps.

Whip: To beat rapidly to incorporate air, increase volume or thicken.

Oven Temperatures

	CELSIUS	FAHRENHEIT
Very slow	120	250
Slow	150	300
Moderately slow	160	325
Moderate	180 –190	350 – 375
Moderately hot	200 – 210	400 – 425
Hot	220 – 230	450 – 475
Very hot	240 – 250	500 – 525

Dry Measures

METRIC	IMPERIAL
15 g	½ oz
30 g	1 oz
60 g	2 oz
90 g	3 oz
125 g	4 oz (¼ lb)
155 g	5 oz
185 g	6 oz
220 g	7 oz
250 g	8 oz (½ lb
280 g	9 oz
315 g	10 oz
345 g	11 oz
375 g	12 oz (¼ lb)
410 g	13 oz
440 g	14 oz
470 g	15 oz
500 g	16 oz (1 lb)
1 kg	320 oz

Liquid Measures

METRIC	IMPERIAL
30ml	1 fluid oz
60ml	2 fluid oz
100ml	3 fluid oz
125ml	4 fluid oz
150ml	5 fluid oz (¼ pint)
190ml	6 fluid oz
250ml	8 fluid oz
300ml	10 fluid oz (½ pint)
500ml	16 fluid oz
600ml	20 fluid oz (1 pint)
1000ml	(1 litre) 1¾ pints

Approximate Measures

1 measuring cup = approximately 250ml
1 tsp = approximately 5ml
2 tsp = 1 dessertspoon = approximately 10ml
1 tbs = approximately 20ml

Quick Conversions

1 cup	almond meal	= 110g
1 cup	butter, margarine, copha	= 250g
1 cup	dried breadcrumbs	= 100g
1 cup	fresh breadcrumbs	= 60g
1 cup	grated cheese	= 125g
1 cup	coconut	= 90g
1 cup	flour (SR, plain, wholemeal)	= 125g
1 cup	dried fruits	= 160g
1 cup	chopped nuts	= 125g
1 cup	rice, sago, tapioca (uncooked)	= 200g
1 cup	split peas, beans, lentils	= 200g
1 cup	sugar (white, caster)	= 250g
1 cup	brown sugar	= 180g
1 cup	icing sugar	= 150g

Guidelines for Cooking Beans, Rice & Pasta

White Rice	¾ cup	Boil 1 litre water and ½ tsp salt. Add rice, simmer 12 minutes. Drain.
Brown Rice	¾ cup	Boil 1 litre water and ½ tsp salt. Add rice, simmer 45 mins. Drain.
Dried Beans eg soy, brown, borlotti, cannellini, haricot	1 cup	Pour 1 litre boiling water and 1 tsp salt over beans. Leave 6 hrs or overnight. Drain. Bring to boil in fresh water. Simmer until tender (1-2 hrs). Drain.
Pasta & Noodles	1½ cups	Boil 1 litre water and ¼ tsp salt. Add pasta, simmer 15 mins. Drain.

Lentils	1 cup	Bring to boil in 1 litre water and ½ tsp salt. Simmer 15-20 mins until tender. Drain.
Chick Peas	1 cup	Pour 1 litre boiling water and ½ tsp salt over chick peas. Leave for 24 hours. Drain. Bring to boil in fresh water. Simmer 2-2½ hrs.

Note: All of the above quantities yield approximately 2 cups when cooked.

Temperature Guide & Roasting Times

LAMB

METHOD	CUT	TIME	TEMP.
Boil & Simmer	Leg – plain	Place in boiling water. Reduce heat and simmer for 60 mins per kg.	
	Leg – cured or pumped	Place in cold water and bring to the boil. Reduce heat and simmer until tender.	
Soup	Shanks, scrag neck	2 hours min	Med-low
	Mutton, hogget	2½ hrs	Med-low

METHOD	CUT	TIME	TEMP.
Tongue		2-3 hrs or until tender	Med-low
Roast		60 mins per kg. If seasoned add extra 30 mins.	160-180°C
Grill, fry or BBQ		Grill: 12-16 mins Fried: 8-12 mins Plain, crumbed or BBQ'd 8-15 mins (depending on BBQ)	High-med, turn often
Casserole braise & stew		1½ hrs Gentle simmer	Med-low

BEEF

Grill, fry or BBQ Steak		Grill: 7-15 mins Fried: 10-20 mins Hotplate: 7-15 mins BBQ: 7-20 mins (depending on BBQ)	High-med

METHOD	CUT	TIME	TEMP.
Casserole braise & stew Steak		4 servings – 2hrs	Med-low
Simmer Large cuts		80 mins per kg	Med, steady simmer
Soup Brawn		2 hours min	Med, steady simmer
Roast Large or thick cuts		Roast 60 mins per kg 40 mins per kg for medium rare	160-180°C

PORK

METHOD	CUT	TIME	TEMP.
Roast Large thick cuts	Leg – loin	100 mins per kg	160-180°C
	Boned rolled shoulder, foreloin or cushion	80 mins per kg	

METHOD	CUT	TIME	TEMP.
	Spring or belly (rolled)	90 mins per kg	160-180°C
Grill, fry or BBQ Remove rind *before* cooking	Butterfly steak	5-20 mins	Moderate, turn often
	Leg steaks. Forleloin steak	10-15 mins	
	Chump chops, forequarter chops, loin chops	15-20 mins	
Braise or stew Steak		3-5 mins to brown 20-40 mins in sauce	Moderate
Boil & simmer		60 mins per kg	Place in cold water bring to boil. Reduce heat & simmer

VEAL

METHOD	CUT	TIME	TEMP.
Roast		80 mins per kg 90 mins per kg if rolled and filled with seasoning	160-180°C
Grill, fry, braise, casserole		Fried: 5-10 mins Grill: 7-10 mins 10-15 mins Casserole: 1-1½ hrs	High-medium, down to medium
Stew	Knuckle neck	1½ hrs	Medium, steady simmer
Soup	Shank	1½ hrs	Medium, down to low

POULTRY

METHOD	CUT	TIME	TEMP.
Roast whole	Turkey	3-3½ hrs 5-6kg bird 4-4½ hrs 6½-8kg bird	160°C on a stand
	Goose	50 mins per kg	180°C on a stand
	Duck	40 mins per kg	160°C on a stand or rack
	Quail	20-30 mins per kg	160°C on a stand in dish or Vertical rack
	Chicken	60 mins per kg	160°C on a stand in dish or Vertical rack
Grill, fry		10-15 mins	Low-med

METHOD	CUT	TIME	TEMP.
Braise, stew or casserole	Any without bone	Serving 4: 1-1½ hrs depending on piece	Moderate heat, gentle simmer
Steam or simmer	Whole fowls bone gentle	Age will determine cooking. Minimum 1½ hours, test for tenderness	Simmer or steam over steadily boiling water
Soups	Neck, carcase, giblets	Cold water, bring to boil. Reduce to low	Gentle simmer

Breakfast

Breakfast is the most important meal
of the day. These simple and healthy dishes
can be made in minutes and will give you all
the energy you need to start your day.

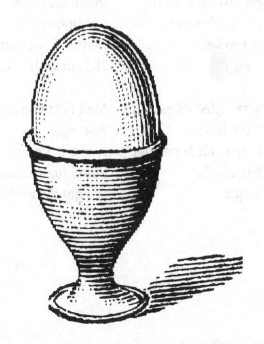

Easy Eggs Three Ways

Soft boiled eggs: place eggs in boiling water and cook for 3 minutes.

Hard boiled eggs: place eggs in boiling water and cook for 10 minutes.

Poached eggs:
Enough water to cover your saucepan to 5cm depth
½ tsp vinegar
¼ tsp salt
1 egg

Bring water to simmer, add vinegar and salt. Break egg into a cup and gently slide into a saucepan. Continue to simmer for 2-3 minutes, until set. Lift out with a slotted spoon.

Scrambled eggs:
1 tsp butter
Pinch salt & pepper
2 tbs milk
1 egg

Melt butter in a saucepan. Beat egg. Add salt, pepper and milk. Pour into a saucepan. Stir gently until mixture thickens.

Traditional Omelette

2 eggs
2 tbs water
2 tsp butter
Salt & pepper

Suggested Fillings:
1 tbs cheese, grated
1 tbs spring onions
or chives, chopped
1 rasher bacon,
chopped & fried
2 tbs ham, chopped
1 medium tomato,
peeled & diced
together with pinch
Salt & pepper
½ avocado, peeled
& sliced
½ cup chicken,
cooked & diced

Separate egg whites from egg yolks.
Add pepper and water to yolks, beat until creamy.
Beat egg whites, add a pinch of salt and continue beating until stiff.
Fold egg yolks into egg whites.
Melt butter in a pan, pour in egg mixture. Cook over gentle heat until golden brown underneath and beginning to set on top.
Sprinkle your filling of choice over the top.
Run a spatula around the edges to loosen.
Fold in half.
Cook for another 1-2 minutes on each side.

Egg & Ham Breakfast Muffins

Canola oil spray
4 wholegrain muffins, halved & toasted
120g leg ham, shaved
4 eggs
4 slices tasty cheese

Spray frying pan with oil.
Heat over medium heat.
Cook ham, turning, for 2-3 minutes or until light golden.
Transfer to a plate.
Cover to keep warm.
Preheat grill on medium.
Lightly spray pan with oil.
Heat over medium heat.
Cook eggs for 4 minutes or until cooked to your liking.
Place 4 muffin halves on a baking tray lined with foil.
Place 1 egg on each muffin.
Top each with ham and 1 slice cheese.
Grill for 1 minute or until cheese has melted.
Top with remaining muffin halves.

Breakfast Museli Muffins

2 eggs
1 cup buttermilk
¼ cup light olive oil
2 tbs honey
2 cups muesli
(toasted with dried
fruit)
1¼ cups plain flour
½ tsp bicarbonate
of soda
1 orange

Preheat oven to 200°C.
Line a 12-cup muffin pan with
paper cases.
Whisk eggs, buttermilk, oil
and honey together. Combine
muesli, flour and soda in a
bowl.
Finely grate orange rind into
dry ingredients. Juice the
orange and add ½ cup of the
juice to egg mixture.
Pour wet ingredients into dry
and mix together quickly
using a wooden spoon until
just combined. Mixture may
be lumpy and does not have
to be evenly mixed.
Spoon mixture into paper
cases. Bake for 20 minutes
or until golden and cooked
through. Cool for 5 minutes
before transferring to a wire
rack to cool completely.

Bircher Muesli with Fruit

1 cup rolled oats
½ cup apple juice
½ cup apple, grated
¼ cup natural
yoghurt
Juice of ½ a lemon
¼ cup mixed
berries

Place oats and apple juice in a bowl and soak for 1 hour, or overnight.
Add grated apple, yoghurt and lemon juice to oats and mix well.
Spoon into bowls and top with fresh berries.

"For a refreshing change in summer top with mango and passionfruit."

Porridge with Banana & Pecan Topping

1 cup rolled oats
1 cup milk
1 cups boiling
water
Pinch of salt
½ large banana,
chopped
2 large dates,
chopped
¼ cup pecans,
toasted, chopped
½ tbs maple syrup

Combine oats, milk, boiling water and salt in a saucepan.
Place over medium heat.
Cook, stirring with a wooden spoon, for 5 minutes or until porridge comes to the boil and thickens (it should coat the spoon).
Remove from heat.
Cover and stand for 10 minutes (porridge will cool and thicken slightly on standing).
Spoon porridge into bowls.
Top porridge with banana, dates and pecans.
Drizzle with maple syrup. and serve.

Avocado Toast with Lime & Pepper

1 tbs lime juice
1 tbs olive oil
Sea salt & pepper
**1 avocado, peeled
& sliced**
**2 slices sourdough
bread, toasted**
Coriander

Place lime juice, olive oil, salt and pepper in a bowl and whisk until combined. Place slices of avocado on toast, drizzle lime dressing over the top. Sprinkle coriander over the top and serve.

French Toast with Strawberries

2 eggs
⅓ cup milk
Butter, melted
4 slices white bread,
thickly cut
1 punnet
strawberries
Vanilla yoghurt
Maple syrup

"Replace the white bread with fruit bread for extra sweetness."

Use a fork to whisk together the eggs and milk in a bowl. Heat a non-stick frying pan over medium heat. Brush with melted butter to lightly grease. Dip 1 slice of bread into egg mixture to evenly coat. Cook for 2 minutes each side or until golden. Repeat, in 3 more batches, with the remaining bread and egg mixture, greasing and reheating pan between batches. Top with strawberries, yoghurt and maple syrup to serve.

Banana Smoothie

1 cup milk
1 tbs natural yogurt
1 tsp of honey
1 ripe banana

Place all the ingredients in a blender and process until smooth.
Serve immediately.

"Add extra zest by adding an egg or some wheatgerm. Try other fruits in season like mangoes, strawberries, peaches, apricots or a combination of these fruits."

Fresh Fruit Crush

125g strawberries
1 chopped banana
Flesh of 1 mango
Flesh of 1 peach
3-4 fresh mint
leaves
4-6 ice cubes

Place all the ingredients in a blender and process until smooth.
Serve immediately.

Fresh Fruit Crush

1½ c. strawberries
1 chopped banana
Flesh of 1 mango
Flesh of 1 peach
3-4 fresh mint
leaves
8 ice cubes

Place all the ingredients
in a blender and process until
smooth.

Serve immediately.

Starters

These tasty dishes are great to have at the start of a meal or on their own for an afternoon snack with your favourite beverage.

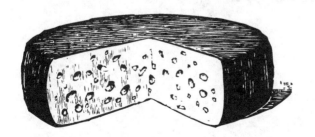

Cheese Dip

125g pkt cream cheese
¼ cup mayonnaise or sour cream
2 tsp lemon juice

Suggested Fillings:
1 avocado and a splash of tabasco
A can of smoked oysters, drained & lightly mashed
A packet of French onion soup mix
½ cup semi sundried tomatoes, finely chopped

Mix all the ingredients together.
Add one of the suggested fillings.

Cheese Strudel

250g cottage or ricotta cheese
125g tasty cheese
2 tbs sour cream
2 eggs
½ bunch shallots
Salt & pepper
Cayenne pepper
Sheet puff pastry

Mix cheese, sour cream, eggs, shallots and seasoning.
Spread filling over pastry leaving room to fold and seal.
Brush edges with egg yolk and bake in a moderate oven for 30 minutes.

Salmon Patè

1 tbs gelatine
½ cup hot water
1 chicken stock
cube
250g tin red salmon
¼ cup mayonnaise
2 tbs parsley sprigs
3-4 tsp lemon juice
2 shallots
½ cup cream
Salt & pepper

Put hot water, gelatine and stock cubes into blender, blend on high speed for 2 minutes.
Add undrained salmon, chopped shallots and all remaining ingredients except cream.
Blend until smooth.
Fold very lightly whipped cream through.
Refrigerate in mould or serving dish until set.

Brandy Patè

90g butter
1 medium onion, chopped
250g chicken livers, trimmed & cut in half
½ tsp thyme
1 clove garlic, peeled & crushed
1 bay leaf
2 tsp sherry or brandy
Salt & pepper
Parsley to serve

Heat butter, add onions and fry for a few minutes.
Add livers, thyme, garlic, salt and pepper and a bay leaf.
Cook until livers are just brown (approximately 5 minutes).
Cool slightly.
Remove bay leaf and place liver mixture in a blender, add brandy and puree to a cream.
Put into a serving dish.
Finish with melted butter and a sprig of parsley.

Pears with Blue Vein Cheese

2-3 pears
125g blue vein
cheese
¼ cup cream
cheese, softened

Cut pears in half, remove core with a teaspoon. Mix the cheeses together. Fill pears with cheese the mixture.

"Replace the pears with fresh figs or mayonnaise instead of cream cheese."

Sausages with Honey Mustard Sauce

Sausages
3 tbs honey
1 tbs seeded
mustard

Grill sausages and pat with a paper towel to remove excess fat.
Cut into 40cm lengths.
Mix honey and seeded mustard together.
Add sausages and coat.

Grapefruit & Pineapple Cocktail

Grapefruit
Pineapple
Caster sugar
Sherry
Mint

Remove flesh from grapefruit and skin from pineapple.
Cut into cubes.
Sprinkle with a little caster sugar and sherry.
Chill for several hours.
Put into champagne bowls.
Decorate with a sprig of mint.

Pineapple Mint Cocktail

1 fresh pineapple
2 tbs caster
3 tbs sherry
1 tbs chopped mint
Strawberries to serve

Peel, core and dice the pineapple.
Sprinkle with caster sugar and sherry.
Toss in chopped mint.
Pour into glasses, top with mint leaf and strawberries.
Chill.

Brandied Grapefruit

2 grapefruits, halved
8 tbs light brown sugar
4 tbs brandy

Loosen flesh and remove seeds of grapefruit.
Sprinkle each half with 2 tbs of sugar and 1 tbs of brandy.
Marinate for ½ hour.
Bake in a moderate oven until hot and bubbling.
Serve hot.

Open Pumpkin & Feta Pies

350g pumpkin, peeled & cut into 1cm cubes
2 tsp olive oil
Salt & pepper
3 sheets frozen puff pastry, thawed
2 eggs
100ml light thickened cream
100g feta, crumbled

Preheat oven to 200°C.
Grease 2 x 12-hole muffin pans.
Place pumpkin on a baking tray lined with baking paper.
Drizzle with oil and season with salt and pepper.
Roast for 20 minutes or until cooked.
Cut 20 rounds from the pastry sheets using a 6.5cm cutter. Press into muffin holes to cover base and a little of the sides.
Whisk eggs and cream together.
Divide pumpkin among rounds, top with 1 tsp of egg mixture, then sprinkle with feta.
Bake for 15-20 minutes until golden.
Cool slightly, then turn out.

Cheese Quesadillas with Guacamole

Olive oil cooking spray
6 flour tortillas
½ cup cheddar cheese, grated

Guacamole
3 avocados, halved & roughly chopped
1 small red onion, finely chopped
1 long red chilli, deseeded & finely chopped
¼ cup coriander, chopped
¼ cup lime juice

Spray a frying pan with oil. Heat over medium heat. Place 1 tortilla in pan. Sprinkle 2 tbs of cheese over tortilla.
Top with another tortilla. Spray top with oil. Cook, pressing down firmly with a spatula, for 1-2 minutes or until base is golden. Flip quesadilla over and cook for another 1-2 minutes. Transfer to a plate. Repeat with remaining tortillas and cheese.
Cut quesadillas into wedges. Serve with guacamole.

Guacamole
Mash avocado in a bowl. Add onion, chilli, coriander and lime juice. Season with salt and pepper. Stir to combine.

Soup

A hearty bowl of hot soup on a warm winter's night is just what the doctor ordered.

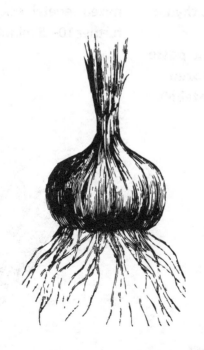

Easy Vegetable Soup

1 cup dried soup mix
6 cups water
1 medium onion, chopped
1 tsp salt
½ tsp dried rosemary leaves
½ tsp dried thyme leaves
140g tomato paste
500g pkt frozen mixed vegetables

Place all ingredients except tomato paste and mixed vegetables into a large saucepan.
Bring to the boil, cover and simmer for 50 minutes or until soup mix is tender.
Add tomato paste and mixed vegetables, simmer a further 10-15 minutes.

Cauliflower Soup

½ cauliflower	Break cauliflower into
3 cups milk	pieces.
3 cups water	Place in a saucepan with
3 chicken stock	milk, water and stock cubes.
cubes	Add butter and salt and
60g butter	pepper to taste.
¼ cup cornflour	Thicken with cornflour
Little milk	mixed with a little milk.
Extra parsley,	Stir until simmering.
chopped	Sprinkle with chopped
Grated cheese	parsley or grated cheese to
	serve.

Pumpkin Soup

2 tbs butter
1 onion, finely
chopped
1 kg pumpkin,
peeled & chopped
6 cups water
2 chicken stock
cubes
1 tsp salt
Pinch pepper
Nutmeg
½ cup cream
Chives, chopped

Melt butter in a large saucepan and fry onion gently until soft and golden.
Add pumpkin, water, stock cubes and salt.
Cover and simmer until pumpkin is very soft.
Allow to cool slightly then puree in a blender.
Add extra salt, pepper and nutmeg if necessary.
Swirl in cream and sprinkle with chopped chives.

Apple & Pumpkin Soup

**2 tsp chicken stock
powder (or two
cubes)
1 onion, diced
500g pumpkin,
cooked & mashed
(preferably
butternut)
¼ cup cream
2 tbs butter
1 granny smith
apple, chopped
2 cups water**

Place butter in a
saucepan add apple and
onion, cook until soft.
Add pumpkin, water and
stock cubes.
Puree.
Add cream before serving.

Quick Short Soup

1 packet frozen
mini wontons
(12-15)
1 egg
Green top of 4
spring onions,
chopped
1 litre chicken stock
2 tsp oil
2 slivers fresh
ginger, chopped
1 clove garlic,
crushed
(or about 1 tsp if
using garlic or
ginger in jar)

Heat oil, add ginger and garlic, stir for 1 minute to release flavour.

Add chicken stock and bring to boil.

Add wontons and simmer for approximately 5 minutes or until wontons are cooked.

Beat egg in a cup with a fork and add to soup, stirring as you pour to make long thin shreds.

Top with chopped spring onions. Serve immediately.

Hint: you can use the commercially prepared packs of chicken stock or tinned chicken consomme; make up to one litre with extra water and one chicken stock cube per cup of water.

Tomato Soup

2 tbs olive oil
1 brown onion, chopped
1 carrot, chopped
2 cloves garlic, chopped
750g fresh, ripe tomatoes, sliced & peeled
400g tin tomatoes
1 litre chicken stock
1 cup water
Salt & pepper
Fresh basil, chopped

Heat oil in a large saucepan.
Saute onion, carrots and garlic for 5 minutes.
Add fresh tomatoes, cook for 5 minutes.
Add tinned tomatoes, stock and water.
Bring to boil, reduce heat and simmer for 30 minutes.
Allow to cool.
Puree until smooth.
Season to taste and sprinkle with basil.

Hint: the best way to remove skin from tomatoes is to slice a cross along the bottom then plunge in boiling water for 20 seconds. The skin should easily peel off.

Cream Corn & Chicken Soup

1 skinless chicken fillet
1 can corn kernels
2 cans creamed corn
2 cups of water
3 chicken stock cubes
1 medium onion, finely chopped
25g butter

Cook onion in melted butter until transparent.
Add corn, water and chicken cubes.
Add chicken fillet that has been cut into thin slices.
Simmer 5-10 minutes

*"Add diced potato or cauliflower that has been broken into very small florets.
Simmer a little longer to make sure the vegetables are cooked."*

Carrot & Orange Soup

50g butter
500g carrots, chopped
1 large onion, chopped
Juice 2 oranges
2 tsp orange rind, grated
1 litre of chicken stock
1 tsp curry powder
1 clove garlic, crushed
Ground pepper
Cream

Heat butter, add onions and carrots. Cook gently for 10 minutes. Add juice, rind, stock, curry powder, garlic and pepper. Simmer 10-15 minutes or until carrots are tender. Blend. Add cream to desired consistency. Garnish with cream, orange slice and rind, mint and parsley.

Lentil Soup

50g butter
1 tbs olive oil
½ cup carrots, chopped
½ cup red onion, chopped
½ leek, sliced (white part only)
½ celery, chopped
4 cloves garlic, finely chopped
1 small chilli, finely chopped
400g tin tomatoes, chopped
1 litre vegetable stock
2 bay leaves
2 tbs fresh oregano, chopped
½ cup green lentils
Salt & pepper
Parsley to serve

Melt butter and oil in a saucepan over medium heat.

Add carrots, onion and leeks, cook for 10 minutes, stirring occasionally.

Add celery, garlic and chilli, cook for a further 5 minutes.

Add tomatoes, stock, bay leaves, oregano and lentils and bring to the boil.

Reduce heat and simmer for 30 minutes, stirring occasionally.

Season with salt and pepper and sprinkle parsley over the top.

Serve with thick crusty bread.

Creamy Mushroom Soup

25g butter
1 onion, sliced
400g field mush-
rooms, chopped
2 cloves garlic,
finely chopped
3 cups beef stock
1 cup water
250ml cream
Salt & pepper
2 tbs parsley,
chopped

Melt butter in a saucepan over medium heat.
Add onions and cook for 2-3 minutes.
Add mushrooms and cook for another 5 minutes, stirring occasionally.
Add garlic, cook for 2 minutes.
Add stock and water, reduce heat and cook for 35 minutes or until mushrooms are very tender.
Remove from heat, blend until smooth.
Return to heat, stir in salt, pepper and parsley.

Main Course

The main course is the heart of the meal. These classic dishes are easy to make and are the perfect dinner for one or a feast with family and friends.

Roast Chicken

1 large chicken
2 tsp oil
2 tsp butter
Salt & pepper

Hint: par boil the potatoes and pumpkin then scrap the surface with a fork before adding to the roasting pan.

Rinse chicken inside and out in running water. Dry well with clean cloth or paper towel.

Season inside and out with salt and pepper.

Close back and neck openings with small skewers.

Tie ends of drum sticks together with string.

Tie wings close to body with string.

Heat oil and butter.

Place bird in baking dish and brush with melted butter and oil.

Bake in a moderate oven allowing 30 minutes per 500g.

Roast Lamb

Potatoes
Pumpkin
Carrots
Parsnips
Onions
2 tbs water

Gravy
3 tbs plain flour
2 cups stock
Salt & pepper

Hint: cooking time is approximately 1 hour per kg of lamb.

Preheat oven to 190ºC.
Peel and cut vegetables.
Place water in baking dish, add lamb. After 15 minutes turn and baste meat.
Add vegetables.
Baste meat and turn. vegetables after 15 minutes. When cooked lift meat and vegetables onto serving dishes and cover with foil to keep hot.

Gravy
Drain all but 2 tbs of fat from baking dish. Add flour, stir over heat until blended and brown. Remove from heat, gradually add stock and stir until smooth. Bring to boil, then simmer a couple of minutes, stirring continuously. Add salt and pepper to taste.

Roast Pork

1½ tbs sea salt flakes
2 tsp dried fennel seeds
2kg boned rolled loin of pork (see note)
1 tbs olive oil
10 small red Gala apples, halved

Note: for ease use a boneless pork leg from the supermarket that comes tied.
If buying from a butcher, ask them to tie it for you.

Preheat oven to 230ºC.
Score skin with a sharp knife if not already done.
Combine salt and fennel in a bowl.
Place the pork, rind-side up, in a roasting pan.
Drizzle the oil over the rind.
Rub the salt mixture over the rind and into the cuts.
Roast for 45 minutes or until the rind crackles.
Reduce oven temperature to 200ºC.
Arrange apples around pork and roast for a further 1 hour 10 minutes or until pork is just cooked through and apple is tender.
Transfer to a serving platter.
Cover with foil and set aside for 10 minutes to rest before carving.

Bianca's Italian Pot Roast

Potatoes
Carrots
A piece of corner topside
2 tbs of butter
2 garlic cloves
2 cloves
2 tbs oil
1 large onion
2 celery stalks
1 sprig of rosemary
2 bay leaves
2 sage leaves
150ml of red wine
1 tbs wine vinegar
½ cup cream

Chop vegetables into large pieces.
Rub meat with some butter.
Cut garlic into pieces and insert into meat.
Place cloves into whole peeled onion.
Place oil, butter, meat, celery, herbs and onion into large saucepan.
Brown meat on all sides.
Add salt and pepper and wine. Simmer for 5 minutes then add vinegar.
Put on lid and cook on low heat for approximately 1-1½ hours depending on size of meat. Meat should cook in these juices, but if more liquid is needed add some stock.
Remove meat when cooked and rest for a few minutes.
Thicken juices with cream.

Beef Stroganoff

750g topside or bladebone steak, excess fat removed
2 tbs butter
2 medium onions, chopped
250g mushrooms, sliced
1 clove garlic, crushed
1 tbs plain flour
1 cup water
1 beef stock cube
1 tomato paste
1 cup sour cream
Salt & pepper

Hint: when coating meat with flour etc, put the dry ingredients in a plastic bag, add the meat, hold top of bag together tightly and shake until meat is well covered.

Cut meat into thin strips. Toss in flour, season with salt and pepper.
Melt butter and fry onions, mushrooms and garlic for 5 minutes.
Add steak and brown (you will need to add about a quarter of the meat at a time in order for it to brown).
Stir in stock and tomato paste.
Bring to a gentle simmer and cook for approximately 30 minutes.
Add sour cream and serve on noodles that have been tossed in butter.
Sprinkle with chopped parsley.
Serve with pasta or rice, add steamed green beans or broccoli.

Steaks in Soy Sauce

500g steak (eg rump)
2 tbs sherry
2 tbs soy sauce
½ tsp ginger, ground
1 tbs oil
1 onion, sliced
2 cups chopped mixed green vegetables (eg celery, sliced green beans, green peppers)
½ cup beef stock
½ tsp sugar
1 tbs cornflour
½ cup toasted almonds
Salt & pepper

Cut steak into thin slices. Marinate in sherry, soy sauce and ginger for at least 1 hour.
Heat oil in frying pan.
Drain marinade from meat and set aside.
Drop in meat a few pieces at a time to seal and cook for 5 minutes.
Add chopped green vegetables and cook for 5 minutes longer.
Add marinade, stock, sugar and salt and pepper to taste.
Blend cornflour with a little water and add to the pan – stir until thickened.
Spoon over freshly cooked rice and sprinkle with toasted almonds.
Serve on rice with tossed salad.

Salmon Casserole

1 cup mushrooms, sliced
1 green pepper, sliced
1 medium onion, chopped
50g butter
1½-2 tbs plain flour
250ml chicken stock
Large tin salmon
1 cup cream

Melt butter then stir in the flour.
Cook 2-3 minutes.
Gradually add chicken stock, stirring continuously.
Season with salt and pepper.
Add cup of cream, flaked salmon, mushrooms and green peppers.
Serve on shell noodles with a side salad.

Spaghetti & Meat Sauce

1 onion, chopped
1 clove of garlic,
smashed
½ kilo mince meat
450g tin of tomato
soup
3 tsp Worcester-
shire sauce
1 tsp paprika
1 tsp cayenne
pepper
2 tsp of olive oil
Salt & pepper

Hint: use a potato
peeler to cut wafer
thin slices from a block
of parmesan cheese.

Heat oil in a saucepan.
Add onion and garlic, cook
until just golden.
Add meat (about a
quarter of it at a time) and
brown.
Stir in can of tomato soup.
Add Worcestershire sauce,
paprika and cayenne pepper.
Simmer on a very low heat
for approximately ¾ of an
hour.
Add salt and pepper to taste.
Serve on cooked spaghetti
topped with grated or
shaved parmesan cheese.

Smoked Trout Pasta Sauce

1 tsp butter
1 tsp crushed garlic
300ml cream
1 smoked fillet of
trout, flaked into
small pieces
Salt & pepper

*"Replace smoked
trout with
diced ham and
mushrooms."*

Melt butter in a small
saucepan.
Add garlic, cook over
moderate heat for 1-2
minutes, stirring to make
sure it does not brown.
Add cream.
Add flaked trout.
Add salt and pepper to
taste.
Pour sauce over cooked
pasta and sprinkle with
shaved parmesan to serve.

David's Marsala Chicken

4 rashers bacon
1 onion
10-12 button
mushrooms
1½ tbs marsala
300ml bottle cream
2 skinless chicken
fillets, diced

Dice bacon, saute in a little butter.
Add finely chopped onion and sliced mushrooms.
Saute until the onion is transparent.
Add diced chicken and brown.
Add marsala and poach the chicken until just cooked.
Stir in the cream.
Serve on noodles with a side salad.

Tasty Lamb Chops

1 kg lamb chops
1 onion, chopped
1 tbs vinegar
1 tbs sugar
1 tbs tomato sauce
1 tbs Worcester-
shire sauce
3 tbs plain flour
Salt & pepper
Approximately ½
cup water

Remove excess fat from chops.
Coat in flour that has been seasoned with sugar, salt and pepper.
Place chops in a greased casserole dish.
Sprinkle with chopped onion.
Barely cover with water.
Mix all the other liquid ingredients together and pour over chops.
Cook in a moderate oven for 1–1½ hours.

Apricot Chicken

2 skinless chicken fillets or other chicken pieces
½ packet French onion soup
1 cup apricot nectar

Place chicken fillets in a greased casserole dish. Sprinkle French onion soup mix over top. Stir in apricot nectar. Cook in a moderate oven for approximately 40 minutes.

"Instead of apricot nectar use the juice from a can of apricots together with some apricot halves."

Scotch Fillet Casserole

2 pieces Scotch fillet
½ packet French onion soup mix
¾ cup water

Place steak in a greased casserole dish.
Sprinkle French onion soup over the top.
Stir in water.
Cook in a moderate oven for 45 minutes.
Serve on mashed potatoes (see recipe on page 104).

Impossible Pie

4-5 eggs
1 small onion, chopped
1½ cups milk
1 cup cheese, grated
¾ cup pastry mix
Parsley, chopped

Suggested Fillings:
1 cup bacon, chopped
1 large can asparagus, drained
1 packet frozen spinach
1 cup mushrooms, sliced
1 tin red salmon

Beat eggs together.
Stir in all other ingredients.
Add one or two of the suggested fillings, stir to combine.
Place in a greased pie plate or a slice tin.
Sprinkle with chopped parsley.
Bake in a moderate oven for 50 minutes.

Cheese & Bacon Casserole

90g cheese, grated
1 small onion,
sliced
2 medium
potatoes, sliced
½ cup milk beaten
with 1 egg
Salt & pepper
6 rashers bacon,
chopped
Parsley to serve

Arrange alternate layers of
potatoes, cheese and
onion in a greased
casserole dish finishing with
the potato.
Add chopped bacon to egg
and milk mixture and pour
over dish.
Bake in a moderate oven for
1 hour or until set.
Sprinkle with parsley.
Serve.

Quick Meatballs

500g lean beef mince
1 zucchini, grated
1 small carrot, grated
1 brown onion, grated
4 button mushrooms, grated
2 tbs parmesan cheese, grated
800g can tomato soup
Parsley to serve

"Leftover meatballs are delicious served in a sandwich the next day."

Preheat oven to 180°C.
Grease a baking dish.
Combine mince, zucchini, carrot, onion, mushrooms and cheese in a bowl.
Roll 1 tbs of the mince mixture into a ball. Place in a prepared baking dish.
Repeat with the remaining mixture.
Top meatballs with tomato soup.
Bake for 30 minutes or until meatballs are cooked through.
Sprinkle with parsley.
Serve.

Pot Roast Chicken

8 chicken portions
2 tbs oil or
butter
1 large onion,
chopped
Salt and pepper
Pinch oregano and
basil
Sprig rosemary
1 cup white wine
1 can of tomatoes
1 cup water

Brown chicken in oil or butter in a large saucepan. Remove chicken from the pan and set aside.
Add the diced onion to the pan, fry until golden.
Return chicken portions to the saucepan together with the salt, pepper, herbs and wine.
Cook for 5 minutes.
Add the canned tomatoes and water, cook slowly for approximately 30 minutes.

Curried Barley & Vegetables

1½ cups pearly barley

200g margarine or butter

2 white onions, sliced

2 cloves garlic, crushed

2 tsp curry powder

½ tsp garam masala

2 large potatoes, cubed

375g pumpkin, cubed

250g green vegetable pieces

4 cups water

Rinse barley and soak for several hours.

Heat margarine or butter in a pan, add the onion and stir until golden.

Add the garlic, curry powder and garam masala, stir over heat for 1 minute.

Add the barley, potatoes, pumpkin and water, cover, bring to the boil, reduce heat then simmer for 10 minutes.

Add green vegetables and simmer for a further 10 minutes or until vegetables are tender.

"Include other vegetables such as sliced carrots, cauliflower and broccoli."

Meat Loaf

500g minced steak
500g sausage
mince
1 onion, finely
chopped
2 cups soft
breadcrumbs
2 tsp
Worcestershire
sauce
½ cup tomato sauce
1 egg
Salt & pepper

Mix all ingredients
together.
Press into a loaf pan.
Bake in a moderate oven for
1½ hours.

Tuna Loaf

¼ **cup spring onions, chopped**
3 tbs butter, melted
440g can tuna
2 cups rice, cooked
2 tbs parsley, chopped
1tbs lemon juice
1tsp salt
Pinch cayenne pepper
2 eggs
Milk

Saute spring onions in butter until soft.

Mix with drained tuna, rice, parsley and lemon juice.

Add salt, pepper, beaten eggs and enough milk to bind mixture.

Press into a greased, foil-lined loaf pan.

Bake in a moderate oven for 40-45 minutes.

Serve cold with a side salad.

Chow Mein

500g lean minced steak
1 tbs oil
1 onion, chopped
1 packet chicken noodle soup
1-2 tsp curry powder
Salt & pepper
1 cup water
3 cups cabbage, finely sliced

Lightly cook onion.
Add meat and brown.
Add curry powder, soup mix and water.
Place cabbage on top of the meat mixture.
Simmer until cooked (approximately 15 minutes) stirring occasionally.
Serve on boiled rice.

"To give a slightly different flavour, or to make a larger quantity, add sliced green beans, chopped celery, pineapple pieces, grated carrot, green beans or sprouts."

San Choy Bau

500g pork or
chicken mince
1 tbs olive oil
1 red chilli, finely
chopped
2 cloves garlic,
chopped
1 tbs soy sauce
1½ tbs oyster sauce
125g bean sprouts
½ cup spring
onion, finely
chopped
6-8 small iceberg
lettuce cups

Heat oil in a wok or frypan.
Add pork or chicken mince,
stir until browned all over.
Add chilli and garlic and stir
for 5 minutes.
Add soy sauce, oyster sauce,
sprouts and spring onion,
stir briefly until combined.
Divide mixture between
lettuce cups.
Serve immediately.

Sausage Roll

2 packets puff pastry, at room temperature
750g sausage mince
1 onion finely, chopped
1 egg yolk, beaten
4-5 slices white bread (trim off crusts)
½ tsp mixed herbs
Salt & pepper

Hint: if you don't have a piping bag, snip the corner of a plastic food bag.

Place bread in a bowl and cover with warm water.
Put sausage mince, finely chopped onion, herbs and salt and pepper into a bowl.
Drain water from bread and squeeze to extract water.
Add bread to sausage mince and mix well.
Pipe sausage mince along the edge of a sheet of pastry.
Roll pastry over top so meat is enclosed.
Trim away any remaining pastry and brush with a little egg yolk.
Cut into required size.
Place on a greased oven tray.
Brush with the egg yolk.
Bake in a hot oven for 10 minutes.
Reduce heat to moderate and cook for a further 15 minutes.

Zucchini Slice

375g zucchini
1 large onion
3 rashers bacon
1 cup cheddar cheese, grated
1 cup self-raising flour, sifted
5 eggs, lightly beaten
Salt & pepper

Grate unpeeled zucchini coarsely.
Finely chop onion and bacon.
Combine zucchini, onion, bacon, cheese, sifted flour, lightly beaten eggs and salt and pepper.
Pour into a well greased slice tin.
Bake in a moderate oven for 30-40 minutes.

"Add a grated carrot or a handful of diced leg ham."

Egg & Bacon Pie

2 sheets puff pastry
1 onion, chopped
5-6 rashers bacon
5-6 eggs
½ cup milk
1 tsp salt
Pepper
Parsley, chopped

Line a deep pie plate with the pastry.
Cover well with chopped bacon.
Sprinkle with ½ tsp salt and a little pepper.
Top with chopped onion and a little chopped parsley.
Break 5-6 eggs over bacon and break the yolks with a knife.
Cover with more bacon.
Cover with ½ cup milk, ½ tsp salt, more pepper and parsley.
Cover filling with pastry and brush with a little milk.
Use a knife to slit the top.
Bake in a hot oven for 10 minutes, reduce the heat and cook for a further 20 minutes.

Veal Schnitzel

500g veal steaks
¼ cup plain flour
1 egg
2 tbs water
3/4 cup
breadcrumbs
1¼ tsp dried
oregano
2 tsb ground sweet
paprika

Place veal between 2 sheets of plastic wrap. Use a meat mallet or a rolling pin to pound meat until 5mm thick. Toss veal in flour, shake away any excess.

Beat egg and water together in a shallow dish. Combine breadcrumbs, paprika and oregano on a large plate.

Dip floured veal into egg wash then coat with the breadcrumb mix.

Fry veal in hot oil until golden brown on both sides. Drain on paper towel.

Serve with mashed potato or a crunchy coleslaw (see recipes on pages 104 & 101)

Vegetables & Salads

This doesn't have to be the boring part of the meal. These healthy vegetable dishes are packed with flavour and are the perfect accompaniment to any dish.

Hints for Preparing Vegetables

Buy vegetables in season – not only is it more economical but they will be fresher.

Prepare vegetables as close to cooking time as possible.

Use your microwave oven for quick and easy cooking of vegetables.

Store vegetables in crisper compartment of refrigerator except for white and brown onions and potatoes.

Store mushrooms in a brown paper bag – not a plastic bag, which will cause them to sweat.

Stuffed & Baked Jacket Potatoes

4 large potatoes
30g unsalted butter
170 ml cream
4 tbs parmesan cheese, grated
½ cup ham, chopped
3 spring onions, finely chopped
4 tomatoes, peeled, seeded & chopped
½ cup olive oil (plus extra to drizzle)
4 tbs tomato sauce
¼ cup white wine vinegar
2 tsp Worcestershire sauce
1 tbs parsley, chopped

Preheat oven to 180°C. Wash potatoes then dry. Wrap each potato in foil, place on a baking tray and roast for 1 hour. Remove from oven and cut a small slice off the top of each potato. Scoop out flesh and place in a bowl with the butter, half the cream, parmesan, ham, shallots and half the chopped tomatoes. Season with salt and pepper and mix together. Pile back into potatoes, drizzle with extra olive oil and return to the oven for 20 minutes or until golden.

Meanwhile, combine tomato sauce, remaining cream, vinegar, Worcestershire sauce and ½ cup olive oil in a bowl. Whisk together to form a sauce, then add the parsley, season with salt and pepper. Serve the potatoes with the sauce.

Creamy Scalloped Potatoes

10g butter, melted
800g desiree potatoes, peeled
2 cloves garlic, crushed
2 tbs thyme
300ml pouring cream
Salt & pepper

"For extra flavour add small cauliflower florets between the layers of potato."

Preheat oven to 200°C.
Grease a deep baking dish with butter.
Thinly slice potatoes.
Place potato slices over base of dish, overlapping slightly.
Mix thyme, garlic and cream together and pour over potatoes.
Season with salt and pepper.
Cover with foil and bake for 35-40 minutes.
Remove foil, bake for a further 30 minutes or until golden brown.

Roast Mediterranean Vegetables

1 red pepper
1 yellow pepper
2 Spanish onions
2 large zucchini
1 large eggplant or
4 baby eggplants, trimmed
1 fennel bulb, thickly sliced
2 large tomatoes
8 cloves of garlic
2 tbs olive oil
Fresh rosemary sprigs
Black pepper
Lemon wedges and black olives to garnish

Preheat oven to 220° C.
Halve and seed peppers, cut into chunks.
Peel onions and cut into wedges.
Cut zucchini and eggplant into large chunks.
Spread peppers, onions, zucchini, eggplant and fennel in a lightly oiled shallow dish.
Cut each tomato in half and place cut side up with the vegetables.
Tuck garlic among the vegetables, then brush with olive oil. Place sprigs of rosemary among vegetables, grind pepper over top.
Roast for 20-25 minutes, turning vegetables half way through the cooking time.
Garnish with lemon wedges and olives if desired.

Italian Bean Salad

¼ **cup olive oil**
1 small red onion, diced
2 garlic cloves, crushed
1 celery stalk, finely chopped
1 long red chilli, deseeded, finely chopped
400g can borlotti beans, drained & rinsed
400g can cannellini beans, drained & rinsed
2 roma tomatoes, deseeded, finely chopped
¼ **cup parsley, chopped**
1 tbs red wine vinegar
Salt & pepper

Heat oil in a small saucepan over low heat.
Add onion, garlic, celery and chilli.
Cook for 3 minutes or until onion and celery have softened.
Stir in beans.
Cook for 5 minutes or until heated through.
Set aside to cool slightly.
Stir in tomatoes, parsley and vinegar.
Season with salt and pepper.
Serve.

Roast Potatoes

**12-16 small
potatoes
1 tbs extra virgin
olive oil
1 tsp sea salt
Freshly ground
black pepper
1 tbs
rosemary**

Preheat oven to 250°C.
Put unpeeled potatoes into a
pot of salted water and bring
to the boil.
Simmer for approximately 15
minutes, until just about
cooked.
Drain well.
Arrange potatoes on a lightly
oiled baking tray.
Use a potato masher to
squash each potato flat.
Brush with olive oil and
scatter with sea salt, pepper
and rosemary.
Bake on the top shelf for 20
minutes or until crisp and
golden.

Indian Salad

1 cup long grain rice
½ cup sultanas or raisins
1-2 bananas
½ cup salted peanuts
¾ cup mayonnaise
1 tsp curry powder
Salt & pepper

Cook rice and allow to cool. Add sultanas or raisins, sliced bananas and salted peanuts.
Mix curry powder into the mayonnaise and season with salt and pepper.
Pour over rice and toss well. Chill before serving.

Rice Salad

1 cup cold rice, cooked
½ cup celery, finely chopped
½ cup carrot, grated
½ cup red capsicum
½ cup green capsicum
½ cup green shallots
1 tin whole kernel corn
1 tbs salad oil
2 tsp white vinegar
1 clove garlic, crushed
1 tbs mayonnaise
1 hard boiled egg, chopped
Parsley, chopped

Mix oil, vinegar and crushed garlic.
Add salt, pepper and mayonnaise.
Toss in rice and other ingredients.
Sprinkle egg and parsley over top.
Chill before serving.

"Stir through a handful of roast flaked almonds for extra crunch or top with slices of fresh mango for sweetness."

Coleslaw

¼ **cabbage, finely shredded**
1 small carrot, grated
½ bunch shallot, chopped (use some of green stem)
½ red pepper, chopped
½ to 1 small tin pineapple pieces, drained
1 orange, diced
1-2 apples, grated
2 cloves garlic, crushed
1 tsp salt
1 tsp mustard
2 tsp sugar
1 tbn vinegar
2 tbs oil
Some pineapple juice

Combine all the salad vegetables in a serving bowl.
Combine garlic, salt, mustard and sugar into oil, vinegar and pineapple juice. Toss dressing through the salad vegetables.

Potato Salad

**12-15 small
potatoes**
½ cup sour cream
½ cup mayonnaise
**1½-2 tsp seeded
mustard**
Chives, chopped
Salt & pepper

Boil potatoes until cooked
then cut in half.
Blend sour cream,
mayonnaise and mustard,
pour over potatoes while
still warm.
Sprinkle chives over the top
before serving.

*"For an extra creamy
salad add two or three
roughly chopped hard
boiled eggs."*

Tomato & Goat's Cheese Salad

2 flour tortillas
50ml olive oil
¼ tsp cumin, ground
1 cucumber, cut into 1cm pieces
200g punnet red cherry tomatoes
200g punnet yellow cherry tomatoes
2 spring onions, finely sliced
1 tbs coriander, chopped
1 tbs parsley, chopped
1 tbs lemon juice
25g goat's cheese, crumbled
30g pecans, toasted & chopped
Salt & pepper

Preheat oven to 180°C. Slice the tortillas into 1cm strips. Combine cumin and half the oil in a bowl, add tortillas and coat. Place on a baking tray and bake in the oven until golden brown. Place cucumber, tomatoes, onions, lemon juice, herbs and remaining oil in a bowl. Season, then toss to combine. Scatter cooled tortilla chips over the tomato salad. Then top with goat's cheese and pecans.

Classic Mashed Potato

800g pontiac potatoes
40g butter
⅓ cup hot milk
Pinch of sea salt
Extra butter to serve

Wash, peel and chop potatoes.
Cook in a large saucepan of boiling water for 20 minutes or until very tender but not falling apart.
Drain.
Mash potatoes.
Add butter and hot milk.
Mix with a wooden spoon until fluffy.
Season with a pinch of sea salt.

Hint: for an extra smooth mash push the potatoes through a sieve with the back of a spoon instead of using a masher.

Greek Salad

200g feta cheese
1 red capsicum,
diced
2 Lebanese
cucumbers, diced
3 tomatoes, cut into
chucks
1 red onion, thinly
sliced
175g kalamata
olives
½ tbs olve oil
½ lemon

Cut feta into 2cm cubes.
Place capsicum,
cucumbers, tomatoes,
onion, olives and feta in a
bowl.
Drizzle with olive oil and
lemon.

Dessert

Finish your meal on a sweet note with a warm crumble in winter or a cooling custard in summer. These desserts will satisfy any sweet tooth.

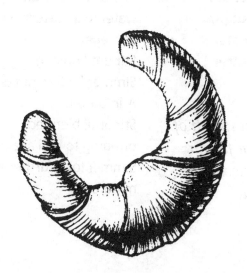

Caramel Sauce

1 tin of sweetened condensed milk
Boiling water

Place a tin of sweetened condensed milk in a saucepan of boiling water for 2 hours.

Chocolate Sauce

½ cup cocoa
½ cup sugar
1 cup water
1 tbs butter

"Add a splash of Kahlua for an extra decadent dessert."

Blend cocoa, sugar and water to a paste in a small saucepan.
Stir until boiling.
Simmer for 3 minutes
Add butter.
Stir until blended, bringing to boil again.
Simmer for a further 4 minutes.

Berry Coulis

250g berries (approximately 1 punnet)
1 tbs water
2 tbs sugar

Place berries and water in a small saucepan and bring to the boil, stirring all the time.
Stir in the sugar.
Push berries through a sieve.
Allow to cool.
Serve with ice-cream, panna cotta or similar dessert.

Basic Custard

1½ tbs custard powder
1 cup milk
1 egg, beaten
2 tsp sugar

"If you want a thicker custard, use extra custard powder.
Add a few drops of vanilla essence for a richer flavour."

Blend custard powder with ¼ of milk.
Heat rest of the milk in a small saucepan until almost boiling.
Pour over blended custard powder, stirring all the time with a wooden spoon.
Return mixture to saucepan.
Stir over heat until boiling.
Reduce heat and simmer for 30 seconds.
Add egg.
Add sugar to taste.

Baked Custard

4 eggs
1 tbs sugar
2½ cups milk
Vanilla essence

Beat eggs and sugar.
Add milk and vanilla essence.
Pour into a buttered pie dish.
Sprinkle with nutmeg.
Bake in a slow-moderate oven for 35-45 minutes.

Hint: if custard or any other sauce goes lumpy, try beating with a whisk.

Baked Apples

1 apple per person
2 tbs water
2 tbs golden syrup
1 tbs butter

Suggested Fillings:
Sultanas
Dates
**Berry jam mixed
with coconut**

Core apple with an apple corer, leaving the apple whole.
Score skin by running a sharp knife around the middle of each apple.
Place apples in a greased baking or pie dish.
Add water, golden syrup and butter.
Bake in moderate-slow oven for 20 minutes or until apples are tender.

Baked Bananas with Orange Caramel Topping

**4 bananas, sliced
diagonally
2 tbs butter
½ cup orange juice
3-4 tbs dark brown
sugar
Plain flour**

*"Sprinkle with
cinnamon and
pour a little
maple syrup on
top or add some
passionfruit pulp
to the orange
juice."*

Roll bananas in plain flour.
Melt butter and put half in
the bottom of an oven-proof
dish.
Add bananas.
Pour over remaining
butter.
Sprinkle with sugar.
Pour over orange juice.
Cover and put in a
moderate oven – turning
bananas after 5 minutes to
coat with syrup.
Bake for 15-20 minutes –
until bananas are cooked
but still firm.
Serve with cream or ice-
cream or on top of French
toast or waffles.

Marshmallow Dessert

**1 large tin
evaporated milk,
chilled**
¾ cup sugar
½ cup boiling water
6 tsp gelatine
1 tsp vanilla
2 tsp lemon juice

*"Add three
teaspoons of
instant coffee to
the boiling water.
Sprinkle crushed
peppermint crisp
or violet crumble
on top of whipped
cream."*

Dissolve gelatine in
boiling water.
Allow to cool a little.
Put evaporated milk in a
basin and beat well,
gradually adding the sugar,
vanilla, lemon juice and
gelatine.
Pour into a lightly greased
mould or bowl.
Chill until set.
Top with whipped cream,
serve with fresh berries,
passionfruit or berry
coulis (see recipe on page
109).

Banana Split

1 banana, peeled & cut lengthways
Place banana slices on a plate.

2 scoops vanilla ice-cream
Top with scoops of ice-cream.

2 tbs chocolate sauce
Drizzle with chocolate sauce.

3 pecans, chopped
Sprinkle with nuts.

Hint: you can use shop bought chocolate sauce or try out the recipe on page 108.

Mango Fool

150g low-fat ricotta cheese
½ cup low-fat vanilla custard
2 large ripe mangoes, peeled & roughly chopped
Almond biscotti to serve

Place ricotta in a food processor.
Process until creamy.
Pour in custard and pulse until just combined.
Transfer to a large bowl.
Wash and dry food processor bowl.
Process mango until smooth.
Reserve ⅓ cup mango puree.
Fold remaining mango puree into the ricotta mixture.
Half-fill 4 x 1-cup capacity glasses with the mango-ricotta mixture.
Spoon over reserved puree.
Cover and refrigerate for 15 minutes or longer, if time permits.
Serve with almond biscotti.

Mango & Raspberry Meringues

125g punnet raspberries
2½ tbs icing sugar
1 cup thick cream
8-12 meringue nests
1 mango, sliced

"Use sliced peaches instead of mangoes."

Place raspberries and 1 tbs of the the icing sugar in a bowl.
Stir to combine.
Using a fork lightly mash raspberries.
Set aside.
In a separate bowl, beat cream and 1½ tbs icing sugar until soft peaks form.
Add ½ raspberry mixture and stir until combined.
Divide cream mixture between meringue nests.
Garnish with mango slices and remaining raspberries.

Pineapple Chiffon Pie

1 small tin crushed pineapple
1 lemon jelly
1 cup evaporated milk, chilled
1 tbs lemon juice
1 cooked pie shell
Whipped cream

Drain pineapple.
Place juice and lemon jelly in a saucepan and heat until jelly has dissolved.
Allow to cool but not set.
Whip chilled milk until stiff.
Add lemon juice, beat again.
Beat in jelly mixture.
Fold in pineapple.
Pour into pie case and chill.
Top with whipped cream before serving.

Chocolate Ripple Cake

**1 pkt chocolate
ripple biscuits
2 tbs sherry or rum
1 bottle thickened
cream, whipped**

Quickly dip one side of each biscuit in sherry or rum.
Spread with whipped cream.
Top with another biscuit.
Repeat process until all the biscuits are used.
Cover the log with whipped cream.
Stand overnight.
Cut on an angle to serve.

Ginger & Pineapple Dessert

1 tin crushed pineapple, well drained
1 pkt gingernut biscuits
1 bottle thickened cream, whipped

Place a layer of biscuits in the bottom of a slice tin. Cover with whipped cream. Spread with half the crushed pineapple. Top with another layer of biscuits then repeat the process. Finish with a layer of whipped cream sprinkled with powdered chocolate. Refrigerate overnight.

Passionfruit Delight

2 packets lemon jelly
2 cups boiling water
2 eggs
3 tbs sugar
2 cups milk
6-12 passionfruit

Add boiling water to lemon jelly.
Allow to cool a little.
Beat eggs with sugar.
Add milk and passionfruit pulp.
Beat in jelly mixture.
Pour into mould or serving dish to set.

Hint: if you have thoroughly greased the mould (spray oil is good) it should turn out fairly easily by just easing the base of the dessert away from the mould with a knife.

If it doesn't come out, quickly dip the mould into a bowl of hot water then turn onto a plate.

Crepes Suzette

60g unsalted butter
⅓ cup caster sugar
1 cup orange juice
1 tsp orange rind,
finely grated
1 packet of French-
style crepes
2 tbs Grand Marnier
Vanilla ice-cream to
serve

Combine butter and sugar in a large pan over low heat. Stir for 2 minutes, until sugar dissolves.

Increase heat to medium-high, add orange juice and rind, simmer and stir for 2 minutes, until sauce thickens.

Heat crepes following packet directions.

Fold into quarters and arrange in the pan.

Spoon hot sauce over crepes. Remove from heat.

Drizzle liqueur over crepes. Use a match to light the sauce (this will evaporate the alcohol).

When flame goes out, serve immediately with ice-cream.

Lemon Sugar Pancakes

2 cups self-raising flour
½ cup plain flour
2 tbs caster sugar
2 ⅓ cups milk
80g butter, melted & cooled
1 egg, lightly whisked
Extra butter, melted
Extra caster sugar to serve
Lemon wedges to serve

Sift flour into a bowl. Add sugar and stir well. Add milk, butter and egg. Whisk until well combined.

Heat a non-stick pan with some of the extra butter. Add ⅓ cup of mixture to each pan. Cook for 2 minutes, or until bubbles appear on the surface. Carefully turn over and cook for 1 minute.

Transfer pancakes to a plate and wrap loosely in a clean tea towel to keep warm. Repeat with remaining batter, greasing pan between each batch.

If you find the pan is getting too hot, reduce heat slightly. Serve pancakes with lemon and sugar.

Stewed Dried Apricots

250g packet dried apricots
¾ cup sugar
Water

Wash apricots, drain, then cover with cold water and stand overnight.
Drain off fluid and add enough water to make up to 2 cups and place in a saucepan with the sugar. Bring to the boil for 3 minutes.
Add the apricots, and simmer gently 5 minutes
Serve hot or cold.

Baked Strawberries with Almonds

2 tbs slivered almonds
½ cup apricot jam
2 tbs Grand Marnier
2 tsp sugar
2 punnets strawberries, hulled

"Serve with cream or ice-cream or try light sour cream with a little brown sugar stirred through."

Toast almonds on an oven tray in a moderate oven for 5 minutes.
Warm jam, Grand Marnier and sugar in a small saucepan.
Arrange strawberries in a shallow oven-proof dish.
Pour jam mixture through a sieved the pour over strawberries.
Sprinkle almonds on top.
Bake in a moderate oven for 5 minutes or until heated through.

Summer Treat

500g fresh summer fruits (eg peaches, plums or apricots)
1 small cup marsala
½ cup rum or brandy
2 tbs sugar
300g savoiardi biscuits

Quarter the fruit and marinate in sugar, rum and marsala for at least 3 hours.
Layer savoiardi biscuits and fruit in a serving dish, finishing with a layer of savoiardi biscuits.
Pour juice over the top.
Cover and place a weight on top (you can use a tin of canned food).
An hour before serving cover with whipped cream and dust with a little powdered chocolate.

Cassata

**2 litre tub
quality vanilla ice-
cream
1 tbs cocoa
½ cup cream
2 cups blanched
almonds, toasted
1 cup mixed dried-
glace fruits (eg
cherries, raisins,
sultanas, pineapple,
apricots)
¼ cup brandy**

Soak dried fruits in brandy
overnight.
Allow ice-cream to soften
but not melt.
Stir in cocoa, whipped
cream, nuts and dried fruit.
Re-freeze.

Strawberry Bavarois

85g sachet strawberry jelly crystals
100ml boiling water
2 tbs strawberry liqueur (optional)
375ml can evaporated milk
150ml thickened cream, whipped to soft peaks
2 tbs white chocolate, grated

Place jelly crystals in a large bowl.

Whisk with boiling water to dissolve, then allow to cool.

Add the liqueur (if using) then add the evaporated milk and use a hand-whisk to beat until thick and frothy.

Pour the mixture into your prettiest serving glasses or dishes and chill for at least 4 hours or until set.

When ready to serve, top each bavarois with whipped cream, white chocolate and strawberries, if desired.

Panna Cotta

300mls cream
150mls milk
3 level tbs sugar
3 level tbs hot water
2 level tsp gelatine
2 tsp vanilla essence

Hint: to prevent a skin forming on custards, cover the surface with plastic wrap.

Put cream, milk, sugar in heavy-based saucepan. Heat gently until almost to the boil, stirring constantly to make sure the sugar is dissolved.
Remove from the heat.
Pour very hot water into a cup, add gelatine and whisk with a fork until dissolved. Add to cream mixture together with vanilla essence.
Pour into a jug to cool slightly.
When cooled to luke warm give mixture a good stir then pour into 4-5 small moulds, or log tin.
Refrigerate until set – about 4 hours.
Serve with berry coulis or chocolate sauce – or both!

Bread & Butter Pudding

8 slices white bread
3 cups milk
3 eggs, beaten
113g brown sugar
85g sultanas
1 tsp vanilla
essence
½ tsp cinnamon
½ tsp salt
Butter
Marmalade
Ice-cream to serve

"Sprinkle chopped walnuts over each layer for an extra crunchy pudding."

Preheat oven to 170ºC. Grease a deep oven-proof dish.

Smear each side of the bread with butter and marmalade then cut into 4 triangles. Place a single layer of bread on the bottom of the dish, overlapping slightly. Sprinkle with sultanas and sugar then make another layer. Continue until all the bread has been used. Sprinkle sultanas and sugar on the top.

Beat milk, eggs, cinnamon, vanilla and salt and pour over bread. Stand for 30 minutes while the bread absorbs the liquid. Place in oven for 30-40 minutes. The top should be golden brown.

Chocolate Pudding

1 cup self-raising flour
2 tbs cocoa powder
½ cup brown sugar
80g butter, melted, cooled
½ cup milk
1 egg, lightly beaten
Thick cream and berries to serve

Sauce
¾ cup brown sugar
2 tbs cocoa powder, sifted
1¼ cups boiling water

Preheat oven to 180°C. Grease an 8-cup capacity oven-proof baking dish. Sift flour and cocoa into a large bowl. Stir in sugar. Combine butter, milk and egg in a jug. Slowly add to flour mixture, whisking until well combined and smooth. Spoon into baking dish. Smooth top.

Sauce
Sprinkle combined sugar and cocoa over pudding. Slowly pour boiling water over the back of a large metal spoon to cover pudding. Place dish onto a baking tray. Bake for 35 to 40 minutes or until pudding bounces back when pressed gently in centre. Serve hot with cream and berries.

Lemon Sponge Pudding

3 tbs plain flour
1 cup sugar
1 tbs butter, melted
3 tbs lemon juice
Rind of 1 lemon
2 eggs, separated
1 cup milk

Mix flour, ½ the sugar, lemon rind, juice, egg yolks and milk.
Beat egg whites with remaining sugar.
Fold into lemon mixture.
Pour mixture into a greased oven-proof dish and place in a pan of water.
Bake in a moderate oven for 45-50 minutes.

Pear & Berry Crumble

4 pears, peeled & cored
500g frozen mixed berries
¾ cup caster sugar
1 cup good quality muesli
½ cup plain flour
60g butter, softened
Vanilla ice-cream to serve

Preheat oven to 200°C.
Cut pears into 8 wedges.
Place in a bowl. Add berries and sprinkle with ½ cup sugar.
Toss to combine.
Line the bottom of a baking dish with the fruit.
Combine muesli, flour and remaining ¼ cup sugar in a bowl.
Add butter.
Using your fingertips, rub into dry ingredients until mixture resembles coarse breadcrumbs.
Scatter crumble mixture over fruit.
Place on a baking tray and bake for 40 minutes or until golden and crisp.
Serve with ice-cream.

Fruit Trifle

A packet of jam rollettes, sliced (about 1cm thick)
Packet of port wine jelly
3 tbs sherry
3 cups custard
Large can sliced peaches, drained
1 punnet fresh Strawberries, cut in half
Whipped cream
Dark chocolate, grated

Make up jelly according to directions and allow to set. Line the bottom of a clear plastic bowl with slices of jam roll.
Sprinkle with 1 tbs of the sherry.
Top with some of the peaches and strawberries. Cover with 1 cup of custard. Repeat until all the jam roll, fruit and custard is used.
Top with whipped cream and grated chocolate.
Chill in fridge before serving.

Oranges in Caramel Syrup

4 (or more) large oranges
⅓ cup caster sugar
½ cup water
1 cinnamon stick
1 tbs Grand Marnier (or brandy)
¼ cup low fat sour cream
1 tbs icing sugar

Combine sugar, water and cinnamon in a saucepan. Stir over heat without boiling until sugar has dissolved.
Bring to boil, simmer uncovered without stirring, until mixture is a dark caramel colour.
Pour caramel over oranges in a bowl and mix well.
Stir in liqueur, cover and refrigerate for several hours (toffee will dissolve in refrigerator) stirring every hour.
Serve with combined cream and icing sugar.

Hint: can be made a day ahead of time.

Biscuits, Cakes & Slices

There's nothing like a batch of home-baked biscuits or a freshly baked cake. This chapter shows you how to make all the classics and includes a few surprises too!

Honey Joys

90g butter
⅓ cup sugar
1 tbs honey
4 cups cornflakes

Heat butter, sugar and honey until frothy.
Add cornflakes and mix well.
Spoon into paper patty cases.
Bake in a slow oven for 10 minutes.

Double Chocolate Chip Cookies

125g unsalted butter, softened
1¼ cups firmly packed brown sugar
1 tsp vanilla extract
1 egg
1½ cups plain flour
½ tsp baking powder
100g dark chocolate, roughly chopped
100g white chocolate, roughly chopped

Preheat oven to 180°C. Line a baking tray with baking paper.
Place butter and sugar in a bowl and beat with an electric mixer until pale.
Add vanilla and egg and continue to beat until just combined.
Sift in the flour, baking powder and a pinch of salt then fold in.
Stir through chunks of chocolate.
Place tablespoonfuls of mixture 4-5cm apart on the tray.
Bake for 15-20 minutes until golden.
Remove from oven and allow to cool a little before removing to a wire rack to cool completely.

Easy Scones Three Ways

Plain Scones:
2 cups self-raising flour
¼ tsp salt
¾ cup milk
1 tbs butter

Fruit Scones:
2 tbs sultanas or dates
1 tbs sugar
Extra tbs butter

Cheese Scones:
Pinch of cayenne pepper
1 cup tasty cheese, grated
Extra tbs butter

Sift flour and salt, rub in butter.
Add milk – enough to make a fairly soft dough.
Knead lightly on floured board.
Grease the edges of a cup or a round cookie cutter and cut dough into shapes.
Brush tops with milk.
Bake in a very hot oven for 8-10 minutes.
Top with thick cream and homemade strawberry jam (see recipe on page 147).

For fruit or cheese scones follow the steps above and add the required fillings before kneading.

Lemon Slice

1 packet crushed plain biscuits
1 cup coconut
Grated rind of 1 lemon
½ can condensed milk
125g butter

Mix all the dry ingredients. Add the lemon rind, condensed milk and melted butter.
Press into a greased tin lined with waxed paper.
Top with lemon icing
Chill.

Lemon Icing
½ cup icing sugar
2 tbs lemon juice

Lemon Icing

Mix icing sugar and lemon juice in a bowl then spread over slice.

Hint: if you don't have a food processor crush the biscuits by placing them in a strong plastic bag and crushing with a rolling pin.

Apple Slice

185g butter
¾ cup sugar
2 eggs
800g can pie apples
1½ cups plain flour
1 tsp
cinnamon
1 tsp mixed spice

Note: if you're having difficulty spreading the batter, put spoonfuls of the mixture on top of the apples, place in a warm oven for a couple of minutes, take out and spread evenly over the apples with a spatula or knife.

Beat the butter and sugar until creamy.
Add the eggs and beat well.
Stir in the sifted flour and spices.
Spread half the mixture in a greased slice tin.
Place the apple on top.
Spread with the remaining mixture (see note).
Bake in a moderate oven for 50 minutes.
Cool in tin for 10 minutes.
Sprinkle with icing sugar and serve with cream.

Chocolate & Coconut Slice

3 wholewheat breakfast biscuits
1 cup desiccated coconut
½ cup caster sugar
1 cup self-raising flour
2 tbs cocoa
150g butter
1 tsp vanilla essence
1½ cups icing sugar mixture
Extra 1 tbs cocoa
2 tbs hot water

Preheat oven to 180°C. Lightly grease a 16 x 26cm baking pan and line with baking paper.
Break up the biscuits and place them in a mixing bowl with the coconut and sugar. Sift over the flour and cocoa, stir.
Melt the butter in a small saucepan over a low heat. Pour over the dry ingredients.
Add vanilla. Mix well.
Spoon the mixture into a prepared pan and press down to level. Bake for 15 minutes or until cooked.
Sift icing sugar and cocoa into a small bowl.
Add the water and stir well. Ice while it's still hot.
Cut into squares to serve.

Upside Down Peach Cake

1 packet orange cake mix
1 tin peach slices
90g butter
¾ cup coconut
½ cup brown sugar

Pour the melted butter into a cake tin.

Sprinkle coconut and brown sugar over the butter.

Arrange the peach slices on top.

Make up the packet cake mix according to directions. Spread over the top of the peaches.

Bake in a moderate oven for 45 minutes.

When cooked turn upside down onto serving plate.

Classic Chocolate Cake

1½ cups self-raising flour
Pinch of salt
1 cup brown sugar
¼ cup boiling water
75g butter
3 tbs cocoa
1 egg
½ tsp vanilla
½ cup milk

Chocolate Frosting
25g butter, softened
1 cup icing sugar, sifted
1 tbs cocoa, sifted

Sift the flour and salt into a bowl.
Add the brown sugar.
Add the cocoa to boiling water, mix into a smooth paste. Add the butter and stir until melted.
Beat egg, milk and vanilla.
Add cocoa mixture and egg and milk mixture to flour. Mix well.
Pour into greased cake tin.
Bake in a moderate oven for 30-35 minutes.
Cool 10 minutes before turning out of tin. When cool top with chocolate frosting.

Chocolate Frosting
Mix all ingredients in a bowl. If necessary add a little milk to get the right consistency.

Spiced Apple Cake

**2 cups apples,
peeled & diced
1¾ cups sugar
2 eggs, beaten
260g butter, melted
¾ cup raisins
1 cup walnuts,
chopped
2½ cups plain flour
1 tsp bicarbonate
soda
1 tsp mixed spice**

Hint: if a cake is cooked
a skewer inserted into
the centre will come
out clean.

Combine the apple,
sugar, eggs, butter, raisins
and walnuts in a large
bowl until just mixed.
Sift in the flour,
bicarbonate of soda and
spice.
Quickly stir into the fruit
mixture until well
combined.
Pour into a greased
and base-line round or
square cake tin.
Bake in a moderate oven
for 1¼ hours or until
cooked.
Cool in the tin for 10
minutes.
Turn out and serve warm
or cold dusted with
icing sugar and with
pure or whipped cream.

One Bowl Chocolate Brownies

125g unsalted butter
200g dark chocolate, chopped
¾ cup brown sugar
1 tsp vanilla essence
1 cup plain flour
3 eggs, lightly whisked
½ cup dark choc bits
½ cup pecans, chopped

"For an extra chocolate boost, add white or milk choc bits."

Preheat oven to 180°C.
Line a 20cm square cake tin with non-stick baking paper.
Melt butter and chocolate together in a medium saucepan over low heat.
Stir in brown sugar and vanilla.
Add flour and eggs and beat with a wooden spoon until well combined.
Stir in choc bits and nuts.
Pour into prepared tin and smooth surface.
Bake for 40 minutes until set.
Remove from oven.
Cool in tin for 5 minutes then transfer to a wire rack.
Cut into squares to serve.

Something Extra

This chapter shows you how to whip up all
those sides, sauces and preserves for
every occasion.

Herb Butter

4 tbs butter
1 clove garlic,
crushed
½ tsp mixed herbs
or oregano

Soften the butter.
Mix in al the other
ingredients.

*"Spread on thick
cut toast for herb
bread or add the
juice of one lemon
and a little salt
and pepper and
pour over steamed
vegetables."*

White Sauce

1 tbs butter
2 tbs flour
1 cup milk
Salt & pepper

"Use white sauce as a savoury filling in vol au vents. Add a pinch of curry and some drained and flaked red salmon or mushrooms and cooked diced bacon."

Melt the butter in a pan.
Remove from heat.
Add the flour and stir until smooth.
Return to a gentle heat and cook for 1 minute, stirring well.
Add the milk, stirring until smooth.
Bring to the boil and allow to thicken.
Add salt and pepper to taste.

Traditional Gravy

30g butter
2 tbs flour
3 cups chicken stock
1 tbs sherry
Salt & pepper

Pour off the excess meat drippings from roasting pan, leaving ½ cup.

Add butter to a pan and melt on medium heat.

Stir in the flour and cook for 3 minutes, scrapping off any crusty pieces, until light brown.

Add the stock and simmer, stirring for 3 minutes, until thickened.

Stir in the sherry and season with salt and pepper.

Pour into jug to serve.

Basil Pesto

1½ cups fresh basil leaves
⅓ cup pine nuts
2 garlic cloves, chopped
½ olive oil
⅓ cup parmesan cheese, finely grated
Salt & pepper

Process the basil, pine nuts and garlic until smooth. With motor running slowly add oil until all is combined. Transfer to a bowl. Add the parmesan. Season with salt and pepper, stir to combine. Mix through fresh cooked pasta to serve.

Basic Mayonnaise

**4 egg yolks, at
room temperature
2 tbs lemon juice
200ml light olive oil
200ml olive oil
White pepper**

Place the egg yolks, 1 tbs of lemon juice and a pinch of salt in a food processor. Process until the mixture starts to thicken.

Combine the oils in a jug. With the blender motor running, add oil the mixture in a thin, steady stream, scraping bowl with a spatula occasionally, until mixture is thick and creamy. Add the remaining lemon juice.

Season with pepper. Process to combine. Transfer the mayonnaise to a small, airtight container. Place plastic wrap on the mayonnaise surface to prevent a skin forming. Cover and keep in the fridge for up to 1 week.

Strawberry Jam

3kg strawberries, hulled & halved
3kg white sugar
Juice of ½ a lemon

Wash and sterilise jars and lids.

Place strawberries in a saucepan and stir through sugar.

Leave for 1-2 hours while sugar softens the fruit.

Add juice and cook over medium heat, stirring constantly until fruit is soft.

Remove ⅓ of the fruit.

Set aside.

Cook remaining mixture until fruit is mostly dissolved and jam coats the back of a spoon.

Divide the reserved jam between jars then fill with jam.

Allow to cool then seal the lids.

Note: Makes 6 x 330g jars.

Chocolates

125g butter
¾ cup icing sugar
2 heaped tsp instant coffee
¾ cup rolled oats
¾ cup coconut
200g cooking chocolate
Walnut pieces
Glace cherries

Cream butter and sugar.
Add coffee, coconut and rolled oats.
Mix well and roll teaspoonfuls of mixture into balls.
Stand in fridge.
Melt chocolate in double saucepan over boiling water.
Dip balls in chocolate and top with walnut or cherry.

Chocolate Truffles

1 packet crushed Marie biscuits
2 tbs cocoa
1 tin sweetened condensed milk
Vanilla or rum to flavour
½ cup coconut *or*
½ cup chocolate sprinkles

Mix all ingredients except coconut or chocolate sprinkles.
Roll into balls then roll through coconut or chocolate sprinkles.
Chill.

Chocolate Fruits

Strawberries
Mandarin
segments
Lychees
Grapes
100g cooking
chocolate
10g copha

Melt cooking chocolate
with copha in top of double
boiler.
Remove from heat and cool.
Dip fruit into chocolate to
coat all or part of the
surface.
Place on foil-lined tray to
set.

Apricot Balls

300g dried apricots, finely chopped
3 cups coconut
400g tin sweetened condensed milk
¼ cup icing sugar, sifted

Mix apricots, coconut and condensed milk until thoroughly combined. Roll 2 tsp of mixture into a ball. Toss in icing sugar. Keep covered in refrigerator.

Index

		QTY
I Can't Cook Book	$19.99	....
Postage within Australia (1 book)	$5.00	....
Postage within Australia (2 or more books)	$9.00	....

TOTAL* $_____

* All prices include GST

Name: ....

Address: ....

....

Phone: ....

Email Address: ....

Payment:

❏ Money Order ❏ Cheque ❏ Amex ❏ MasterCard ❏ Visa

Cardholder's Name:...

Credit Card Number: ....

Signature: ....

Expiry Date: ....

Allow 21 days for delivery.

Payment to: Better Bookshop (ABN 14 067 257 390)
PO Box 12544
A'Beckett Street, Melbourne, 8006
Victoria, Australia
betterbookshop@brolgapublishing.com.au

BE PUBLISHED

Publishing through a successful Australian publisher. Brolga provides:
- Editorial appraisal
- Cover design
- Typesetting
- Printing
- Author promotion
- National book trade distribution, including sales, marketing and distribution through Macmillan Australia.

For details and inquiries, contact:
Brolga Publishing Pty Ltd
PO Box 12544
A'Beckett St VIC 8006

Phone: 03 9600 4982
bepublished@brolgapublishing.com.au
markzocchi@brolgapublishing.com.au
ABN: 46 063 962 443